S0-BCA-547

BALI

Text by
Prof. Dr. **IDA BAGUS RATA**

Photos by
ANDREA PISTOLESI

BONECHI

BALI
Project and editorial conception: Casa Editrice Bonechi
Editorial director: Monica Bonechi
Picture research: Sonia Gottardo
Graphic realization and videolayout: Sonia Gottardo
Editing: Patrizia Fabbri, Simonetta Giorgi

Text: Prof. Dr. Ida Bagus Rata
Translation: Diane Melville
Map: Studio Grafico Daniela Mariani - Pistoia

©   by Casa Editrice Bonechi

E-mail: bonechi@bonechi.it - Internet: www.bonechi.it

All rights reserved.
No part of this book may be reproduced without the written permission of the publisher.

Printed in Italy by Centro Stampa Editoriale Bonechi.

The cover, layout and artwork by the Casa Editrice Bonechi *graphic artists*
in this publication are protected by international copyright.

Photos by Andrea Pistolesi.
The photographs produced by I. B. Gustra (24 above, 32 below, 117 below)
and Joe Rosarius (page 123) belong to the Bonechi Archive.

ISBN 88-8029-580-2

* * *

INTRODUCTION

*B*ali is a mountainous island of volcanic origin. Its highest peak is Mount Agung (3142 meters), a volcano which has enjoyed long periods of inactivity.

With a surface of 5632 sq. km. and a population of 3 million, Bali is one of the 27 provinces which make up the Republic of Indonesia.

Situated between Java to the west and Lombok to the east, Bali has always been a bridge between Asia and Australia. This has weighed heavily on the island's historical vicissitudes and cultural identity, often forcing Bali to compare itself with other influential nations such as India and China.

The first signs of the "Indianization" of Bali can be directly or indirectly traced back to the VIII Century, at the hands of India, with the mediation of Java.

The first documents to speak of a Balinese ruling dynasty, politically dependant on Java, date back to the X Century. At the end of the 13th Century, Bali was forced to acknowledge the temperary sovereignty of the Javanese kings of Singhasari. This was followed in 1343 by submission to the kingdom of Madjapahiut, named after the dynasty which succeeded the previous one in Bali.

The Javanese influence, thus, continued to be strong and constant and was even greater between the XV and XVI Century because of the massive influx of Hindus who had escaped the forceful dissemination in Java of the Islamic religion and who sought refuge and asylum in Bali.

At the end of the 17th Century, the descendants of the princes of Madjapahit subdivided the island into nine independent principalities; it became a Dutch protectorate in 1743. Actually, Holland had established its commercial settlements in Bali since 1597 but the island fell under its full control only in the mid-19th Century when forms of political and administrative autonomy were suffocated.

Later, as we have seen, Bali became a part of Indonesia although it conserved its own social, cultural and religious characteristics.

In Indonesia, in fact, the majority of the population (approximately 192 million people) is Muslim. Responsible for the dissemination of this religion was the massive and influential presence of the Arabs who had established there an important commercial center and many profitable markets.

When the Indonesian sovereign princes converted to this new faith (XV Century), the majority of the Hindu followers sought refuge in Bali where they were able to maintain their beliefs.

This is why today approximately 93% of the Balinese are Hindus. Muslims, Protestants, Catholics and Buddhists are only a small minority.

There are still strong traces of what must have been the oldest and most primitive form of religion in Bali - animism which is based on the respect for all things and all creatures because they are all equally governed by a spiritual entity or by the soul.

Peaceful coexistance and tolerance have always traditionally characterized the relationship between the various religions. This is best exemplified in Denpasar, capital of Bali, where temples and other areas of worship of the various religions are peacefully built near eachother. It is not surprising, therefore, that Bali is known as the "Island of the Gods", or "Island of a Thousand Temples". Nonetheless, Hinduism best embodies the customs and even the very landscape of the island.

The Hindu areas of worship are found all over Bali (called Pura). Each village (Desa Adat, in the local language) has at least three main shrines known respectively as Pura Desa, Pura Puseh, and Pura Dalem. These places of worship are consacrated to the three divinities which form the Hindu Sacred Trinity or Trimurti, expression of the power of the supreme creator Ida Hyang Widi: Brahma, the creator, Wisnu, the preserver, and Siwa, he who destroys the universe and brings everything back to the primordial elements that compose it, and in so doing, concludes each cycle of creation.

Then there are the Pura Ulunsuwi or Pura Subak. Located in the center of the rice fields and cared for by those farmers who, by using the same source of water, form a type of cooperative called Subak. There is also the Pura located near the traditional markets, called Pura Melanting, for the sellers. And lastly, the Kahyangan Jagat, real public temples, open to the entire population. The Pura Besakih, the largest in Bali, is one of these.

Each Pura has its own "birthday" which, at times, is celebrated once a year, and at others, every 210 days (the equivalent of the lunar year); the ritual celebra-

tion is solemn and attracts crowds of faithful from all over the island. During these occasions, the faithful offer artistic compositions of flowers, fruits, cakes, rice and roast meats as a token of gratitude for the kindness of the divinity, for the abundance granted them and to invoke benevolence for the future.

In Bali, each Hindu family has its own personal sacred temple, the Sanggah or Pamerajan. It is built to honor the venerated memory of their ancestors, the spirits of their relatives and, naturally, Ida Hyang Widi, the only supreme divinity. The Sanggah, in fact, must always look to the sacred mountain, Mount Agung.

As to the island's economy, the major source of income (and the basis of progress and development) is agriculture, the crafts and above all, tourism. The latter started to be developed at the beginning of the XX Century and has undergone a significant and steady growth since the inauguration of the International Airport, Ngurah Rai, at the beginning of the sixties. With the airport, came the first large and modern hotels built to meet the needs of the international clientele.

Agriculture, instead, is still more traditonally based. The most important product is, of course, rice which has been cultivated in Bali for over a millenium. It is indeed considered a gift of the gods and has inspired many legends and mythological tales. Vast rice fields, surrounded by groves of coconut trees occupy the southern planes and the carved sides of hills and mountains, creating the characteristic rice terraces.

In those regions where the climate is dry, rice has been replaced by the growing of maize and tropical tubers often accompanied by the production of fruit and coffee.

On the whole, the vegetation in Bali is thick and luxuriant and the landscape very green. This is just one of the elements that make this island a extraordinarily fascinating and enticing corner of the world, along with the beauty of the sea, its history, the alluring traditions and suggestive ritual ceremonies.

The terraces, essential for the develoment of rice cultivation.

The Barong; two dancers, usually men, move underneath the elaborate costume.

A young Balinese in her typical dance costume.

Previous pages: a classic and monumental gateway (*Candi Bentar*), typical element of Balinese architecture; the outline of the Gunung Agung vulcano, rising between sea and sky.

THE BARONG DANCE

The Barong dance is truly a triumphant display of bright colors and graceful movements. Greatly appreciated by the tourists, special performances are staged for their benefit, generally in the morning, and last one hour.

The villages of Batubulan as well as Tegaltamu and Singapadu, small towns located 30 minutes from the capital, are known for putting on the best performances.

There is, however, more to the Barong dance than the folkloristic dimension. It is, in fact, an integral part of the island's culture and has an evident sacred connotation. It isn't rare, in fact, to see the Balinese

dancing the Barong during their religious ceremonies, regardless of the presence of tourists.

Inspired by an episode taken from *Mahabharata*, an epic poem written in Sanskrit. the dance evolves around the character of the Barong, the king of the jungle. A mythical animal, not clearly identified (perhaps a lion), he is the symbol of virtue and good, subject to the continuous struggle against the evil forces that threaten life and the integrity of the forest, this being an element very dear to the Balinese population.

In detail, the Barong embodies everything that can be beneficial to man, and help him defeat illness,

Opposite page, from left to right, from top to bottom- four typical characters, Dewi Kunti, the stepson Sadewa, here tied to a tree waiting to be sacrificed, a producer of palm tree wine, and Kalika, Rangda's female servant.

Two images of the Barong: above, with a monkey, below, a producer of palm tree wine which he attacked and wounded in the face.

black magic and any other kind of misfortune. The evil entity against which he must relentlessly fight is personified by Rangda, queen of death and devourer of children. She is characterized by a dark and gloomy mask from which a red tongue of fire hangs.

The entire dance is centered around the struggle between these two rival characters. The Barong is interpreted by two dancers whose rhythmic movements bring to life the beautiful and elaborate costume they wear: a large animal head skillfully carved out of wood, brightly colored in red, white, black and gold. It is adorned with a crown extending outwards from the sides of the head, and by a prominent necklace which hangs from the neck. The final touch of the costume is a tail made out of bison leather which is elaborately finished and guilded.

The first character to appear on the stage is the Barong with his swaying gait: his dance is meant to express the joy of living. He is followed by a group of armed supporters who stand ready to defend him

Above, Patih, minister of Dewi Kunti; below, to the left, Rangda, evil spirit, carried on the shoulders of her followers; to the right, two of Patih's servants.

when Rangda strikes her terrible blows. It isn't at all rare for the dancers playing the Barong's followers to become so engrossed in the sacredness of the performance that they go into a real trance.

A cloud of characters surround the Barong on stage: Rangda, goddess of death, personification of evil; the young girl servant Kalika; Dewi Kunti, queen of the kingdom of Hastina and her stepson Sadewa who will be sacrificed in order to placate the anger of Rangda, the minister Dewi Kunti; Patih who expresses sorrow for the fate of Sadewa (Rangda will

have to enter his soul in order to make him accept the sacrifice), and then the monkey supporters of the Barong, producers of palm tree wine (*nira*).

A very important element in the entire dance is the large orchestra, known as *gamelan*, which is essential to underscore the ritual nature of the performance. Many are the instruments that make up the orchestra: some metal xylophones which stand out not only because they are so numerous but because of their powerful and imperious sound; there are also drums as well as flutes, the *rebab* (a type of violin) and the *gender* (typical xylophones). All together, these instruments are essential in guiding the dance and underscoring the rhythm of well coordinated movements. These along with the joyful colors are the most alluring elements of this remarkable performance.

At the end of the dance, the masks of the Barong and of Rangda, as proof of their sacred nature, are stowed in a special room inside the temple. They are covered very carefully, especially Rangda's mask, because its deadly powers are greatly feared. It's a way of saying that the ritual victory of the Barong, that is of good, which marks the end of the dance, is only temporary: tomorrow the eternal and unresolved conflict could begin again.

Two images of the *gamelan* orchestra which leads and accompanies the dance.

15

Under the eyes of the Barong, the Kris dancers, invaded by the evil demon, attempt to stab themselves.

THE KRIS DANCE

The end of the Barong dance is like an entirely separate performance. Also known as the Kris dance, it is named after the famous Malese dagger.

The idea is based on the philosophical concept *rwa bhineda*: good and bad, evil and goodness which have always been present and have always existed together albeit in a constant and inevitably unresolved conflict. Nothing will change in the future. While man is left free to try to develop his positive attitudes and let them win over the negative ones, he must nonetheless resign himself to the fact that the presence of both good and evil is a law of nature and as such must be accepted.

When the dance is performed, Rangda is the evil spirit which enters the bodies of his victirms, usually followers of the Barong, and pushes them to the edge of suicide.

The dancers attempt to stab themselves in the chest with their krises until they are finally stopped by the beneficial appearance of the Barong. It is he who will save these unfortunate beings by revealing that the notion of good and evil will always be inevitablty present in the world and in everyone's life and that they must therefore accept it.

THE KECHAK DANCE

Tourists especially enjoy the performance staged by the Kechak dancers. This dance is also deeply rooted in local tradition and Indian mythology and is inspired by *Ramayana,* an epic poem written in Sanskrit.

The dance brings to life the tale of King Rama, his wife Dewi Sita and his brother Laksamana who were exiled to the forest for 14 years following some complex scheming in a struggle for power.

In the forest, they are persecuted by Rahwana, the ogre king who then abducts Dewi Sita and makes her a prisoner of his palace on the Island of Lanka (Ceylon).

Rama strikes an alliance with the monkey people whose army defeats Rahwana's troups, making it possible for King Rama to rescue his wife.

In each Kechak performance, a hundred or so dancers play the monkey army while a few female dancers are assigned specific roles (Dewi Sita, Trijata). The performance generally lasts one hour and takes place in the evening, preferably around 7 PM.

Below, dancers lying in a circle, mimic the dragon which coils itself around Rama. The king will be saved only by the arrival of the bird Jatayu. To the left, Dewi Sita and Laksamana roam the forest.

Following pages: the army of the monkey people, played by a hundred or so dancers who move rhythmically.

Two typical elements of the Topeng dance: the masks of an old man and of Patih.

Opposite, two different groups of musicians: above, the typical wooden instruments, very similar to cowbells albeit much larger, used to produce a very unique type of music, the *Okokan;* another genre of traditional music, the *Beleganjur* is produced with drums (bottom). Both the *Okokan* and the *Beleganjur* are two musical forms which hold an enourmous appeal during the Festival of Balinese Art, held mid-June to mid-July.

THE TOPENG DANCE

Closely linked to religious ceremonies and processions, and danced as a ritual interval, the Topeng dance ultimately takes on a sacred connotation. As a matter of fact, foreigners are allowed to see the dance only if they behave appropriately and respectfully.

Actually, some performances are staged only for the benefit of the tourists, but do not enjoy the same following of the Barong and Kechak dances.

Peculiar components of the Topeng dance are the masks used to hide the faces of the dancers. Specific attributes are used, instead, to identify the characters (a mustache and thick eyebrows for the elder, arrogance and defiance for Patih, and so on).

The rhythm of movements (perfectly in accordance to the age and role of the character) is underscored by a large orchestra, the *gamelan*, which is essential for the success of the perfomance.

RELIGIOUS CEREMONIES

As previously mentioned, Bali is defined the "Island of a Thousand Temples" or the "Island of the Gods". It is indeed a land interspersed with an incredible number of areas of worship, the only ones where the faithful can engage in a ritual veneration of the ancestors and of Ida Hyang Widi, supreme creator, and his manifestations.

While very numerous, each temple enjoys its own personal birthday (locally called *Piodalan*) which is the date of the temple's first consacration.

The anniversary is regularly and solemnly celebrated during highly suggestive ceremonies, underscored by the attendance of crowds of worshipers.

The rituals last from 1 to 3 days in the case of a temple belonging to a single family, 3 days for a temple belonging to an entire village and from 7 to 11 days for the largest temple in the area, the one that is rightfully the temple of public worship.

During the Piodolan ceremony, each temple is magnificently decorated, as is fitting for a celebration.

The *memendak* is held on the first day; this ritual serves to propitiate the coming of the ancestral spirits and the supreme divinity, Ida Hyang Widi and his manifestations which must remain in attendance at all the following ceremonies.

Hindu devotees come before them in great num-

A sacred area, carefully and elaborately decorated for the *piodalan* celebrations (its birthday).

Following pages: lengthy processions of faithful, with refined attire, headed for the temple, bearing rich offerings which are arranged in monumental and picturesque compositions and which will be neatly placed the in *pelinggih*, the place where the spirits manifest themselves.
Below, a prayer to obtain peace and prosperity.

bers. They arrive in a steady stream, a procession of people clad in elegant garments bearing gifts of flowers, fruits and cakes, all perfectly balanced on their heads and arranged in artistic and picturesque compositions.

After entering the temple, their offerings are placed in the *pelinggih*, the area where the ancestral spirits and the Ida Hyang Widi reveal themselves. If there isn't enough room in the *pelinggih,* the offerings are placed in front of it.

Then, the woman who bears on her head the gifts of her family will pay homage, together with her relatives and a *pemangku* (the priest who officiates the ceremony inside the temple). For this function, the devotee will use flowers and incense.

A demonstration of the Hindu women's ability to balance the encumbersome composition of votive gifts on their head. Opposite, the procession of faithful as they leave the temple after the ceremony.

Above, a *pemangku*, with his assistants dressed in white, surrounded by the faithful who are sitting and are absorbed in prayer while the others balance on their heads the gifts and offering they have come to bear. Below, a *pedanda*, a Brahmana priest with his ritual objects, leads a ceremony to induce the ancestors and Ida Hyang Widi and his manifestations to dwell in the temple's *pelinggih*.

The beautiful gateway to a temple, called *Kuri Agung* or *Candi Kurung*. Worthy of notice are the reliefs which adorn it and wich are masterfully made.

After everyone has prayed, the *pemangku* sprinkles holy water on the heads of the faithful while they drink the water as a sign of having received a gift from the Ida Hyang Widi. As a matter of fact, they will return to their homes bearing their respective offerings which will be consumed by the entire family.

As mentioned, the ceremony will last for several days. A specific ritual, called *ngeluhur*, (return to the eternal residence) marks the closing of the ceremony. It is held to accompany the joyous return of the ancestral spirits and the Ida Hyang Widi to their eternal residence: the sacred mountain.

This important ritual is presided over by another priest, a *pedanda*, who is assisted by the temple's *pemangku*. The successful conclusion of the *piodalan* is directly dependent on the success of this ritual.

Two moments in the cockfight; above, the application of the metal blade; below, the start of the fight.

COCKFIGHTING

Cockfighting is directly associated to the religious ceremonies (called *tabuh rah* or blood sacrifice) and therefore, also acquires a fitting cultural significance.

Especially loved by the Balinese, this event, known as *mecaru,* is really a prologue to the actual ceremony and is viewed as an opportunity to offer spilt blood in order to propitiate Buta Kala (the evil spirit) and keep him from interfering with the religious proceedings that will follow.

Cockfights are, in fact, extremely bloody also because the opposing parties arm the cock's foot with a very sharp metal blade before the fight.

The trainers (*pekembar*) are noisily incited by groups of followers, urging on the fight, possibly to its extreme consequences: either escape or death of one of the contestants.

Although the fight takes place right in front of the temple entrance, amid the enthusiasm of the crowds, there are those who gladly exploit the opportunity to make a profit by taking bets, thus transforming the fight into a form of gambling. This became so popular that the government had to step in and enforce an official ban.

WEDDING CEREMONIES IN BALI

The *pawiwahan* (marriage of a Hindu couple) is a very important part of Balinese social life.

The ritual generally takes place in the home of the groom, a further confirmation of the typical patriarchal inclinations of Balinese culture, and is performed by a priest.

The newlyweds to be, dressed in very colorful and refined garments, worn only for the day of the wedding, will withdraw in prayer in the family temple. This is followed by the presentation of offerings in the *pelinggih* and by a series of ritual gestures.

A very typical moment in the ceremony occurs when the bride offers the groom several different beverages: a conventional way to reiterate that the woman, as a wife, commits herself to obeying her husband and to lovingly care for him for the rest of their lives.

Right, a couple to be wed in their typical costumes, accompanied by two girls, pose in front of the *pelinggih* in the family temple, just before withdrawing for the ritual prayers. Below, the bride offers her husband a beverage in order to reiterate her submission and devotion, in keeping with traditional customs.

The large wooden bullock draped in white and the complex tower which houses the body are being carried in procession from the deceased's family home to the cremation site.
Left, the majestic nine-tier tower, exclusively reserved for the royal family.

CREMATION

Even Hindu funerals in Bali are intensely suggestive ceremonies of great cultural and religious significance.

Requiring a complex apparatus and characterized by a large following, funerals are centered on cremation of the body, known as *ngaben* or *pelebon*. This practice is considered essential if the 5 elements making up the microcosm of the human body are to be returned to their original residence, the universe's macrocosm. The five elements, *Panca Maha Bhuta,* are the earth (*pertiwi*), water (*apah),* fire (*teja)*, air (*bayu*), and ether (*akasa*). Since the primordial dimension can only be attained through water and fire, the ashes are dispersed in the waters of the sea or if the distance is too great, in a river.

The funeral ceremony is generally led by a priest and punctuated by a lavish offering of gifts.

For the occasion, a large bullock-shaped wooden structure is built and then entirely covered with white drapes if the deceased belongs to a priestly caste; in black, if not.

The deceased's body, appropriately placed inside the wooden bullock, burns slowly together with the monumental apparatus.

A huge tower with layered roofs, or *bade* is then prepared with wood and bamboo and very skilfully decorated and colorfully painted (there is a majestic, nine-tier tower which is exclusively reserved for the royal family). The body is placed in the tower and led in procession, along with the wooden bullock, from the home of the deceased's family to the cremation site.

Here, the body is carefully placed in a space carved out of the wooden bullock. The whole structure is set on fire and will continue to burn at length.

The entire population attends the ceremony and participates in its various phases. Even tourists are authorized by the family to assist, provided they behave respectfully.

The cost of such a monumental affair can be exorbitant, especially in light of the fact that tower and bullock are so expertly and accurately made (although they are destined to go up in smoke) that they end up becoming true works of art.

Today, those families who cannot afford the expense tend to opt for a collective ceremony, or alternatively, select a less grandiose and complex apparatus, made out of simple banana tree wood.

A typical Balinese village, surrounded by rice fields and veritable forests of palm trees.

Above and on the following pages: a typical and suggestive Balinese panorama with green terraces where rice is cultivated and rows of palm trees which unwind around the village *Pura* (temple).

RICE FIELDS

A typical component of the Balinese economic structure is the village of farms surrounded by rice fields and groves of coconut trees.

While life there is traditionally agrarian, in recent times the progressive development of tourism has induced an increasing number of farmers to turn to the crafts. From the artists of the various villages, they have learned the secrets of traditional artisan workmanship.

Consequently, the number of painters, carvers, engravers and weavers has grown. Women, instead, are generally involved in the sale of the products of the earth or small home-made items such as clothing.

The Balinese, after all, are a notoriously active and industrious people. Likewise, they have a marked artistic inclination which has been passed on throughout the centuries from one generation to the next.

Profoundly bound to tradition, this population is so devoutly religious that there is little distinction between the material needs of life and the spiritual ones and consequently, it is not surprising to find the village *Pura* surrounded by vast rice fields or an expanse of palm trees.

There are some ritual ceremonies that the Balinese rigourously observe, the most important being *yadnya* which is dedicated to the ancestors and to the supreme creator Ida Hyang Widi. Another five ceremonies (*Panca yadnya*) follow and are dedicated in order of importance to the god (*Dewa yadnya*), to the ancestors (*Pitra yadnya*), to the priest *(Rsi yadnya)*, to mankind (*Manusa yadnya),* to the spirit of evil (*Bhuta yadnya*). Each ceremony is, in conclusion, a harmonious blending of religion, tradition and culture.

The Balinese village inhabitants are traditionally subdivided into different *Banjar*, groups of 50 to 100 families (the family remains at any rate the nucleus of the structure of Balinese society), who are all committed to assisting eachother in the various aspects of social life and to partaking in the periodical communal meetings or consultations which are held in the meeting hall called *Bale Banjar*. Each *Banjar* furthermore boasts a small orchestra which performs traditional music (*gamelan*) and is often accompanied by a veritable artistic troupe, called *Sekaa*.

Ploughing the rice fields with the traditional wooden plough.

Left: a view of the terraces where the rice plants grow and which will later be weeded. Above, a woman busy threshing rice.

WORK IN THE RICE FIELDS

The Balinese preference for a truly communal life style is also reflected in their work and in everyday activities

The farmers or peasants still mainly work the rice paddies according to traditional methods: fields are plowed with a plough pulled by two cows (very few farmers have only recently begun using farm machines considered a bit more useful than one or two cows); they sow the rice and when the plants are grown, the fields are weeded so that the rice will again grow vigorously and luxuriantly.

To do this work, the farmers call in groups of labourers which only recently have begun to receive wages. A more traditional form of payment is based on an equal division of the harvest. It's not surprising considering that farmers and labourers pray together in the temple situated in the center of the rice fields (*Ulunsuwi*) and all share the responsibility of taking care of it. This is yet another example of how the Balinese people endeavor to blend the material and spiritual needs of their lives.

RICE HARVESTING

Harvesting the rice is an extremely complex and important procedure. Though today there are plants equipped with machines that can sift and clean the rice, the family members on the farm still manually perform the various harvesting operations: the men sow, cultivate, plant and harvest. The women likewise take part in the harvest. They also thresh and sift the rice as well as doing the cooking, serving the food, and preparing offerings for the ritual ceremonies.

The main staple food of a farm family is, of course, rice. At times it is served with vegetables, salt and fish. Meat, generally pork, beef, chicken, and duck, is eaten only on special occasions.

Savoury and colorful tropical fruits displayed in a shop.
Opposite, typical *rambutan*.

TROPICAL FRUITS

The feast of bright colors that marks every moment of Balinese life would be incomplete without the very colorful and varied tropical fruits that grow on the island.

The majority come from the most eastern part of Bali, the Karangasem, and are neatly and appealingly displayed in large containers in all Balinese markets.

One can easily find at least a dozen types of bananas in various colors and tasting very differently, along with peculiar tangerines and grapefruits, pomegranates and pineapple as well as rarer varieties: *salak*, a curious clustered brown fruit, mango, *sawo* which looks like a potatoe and tastes like a pear, *blimbing* which is a favorite fruit of the women of Bali, the typical *rambutan*, unmistakably enveloped by flexibile and fleshy thorns, *sirsak*, green and very sweet, papaya, *nangka*, with its thick rough, yellowish skin, and the famous *mongasteen,* a small brown fruit with a very white fleshy core.

This enormous variety of fruit found in Bali makes it possible to create deserts which are as original as they are savoury.

While these fruits are appealing and appetizing for the tourists, for the Balinese they are an important element in the creation of those monumental compositions which are brought to the temples as gifts during the religious ceremonies.

THE DUCK SHEPHERD

A "shepherd" leading a small group of ducks is not an uncommon sight in Bali. They are farmers who raise ducks and sell the eggs and meat at the market in order to bring in some extra income for the family.

Duck is an animal in great demand as an offering during the religious ceremonies. For the Balinese, the duck is sacred because it never fights with other animals and is also very careful in choosing the food it eats; this is especially true of white ducks.

Consequently, in October and April, when the moon is full, and thus the best time for traditional rites, the price of duck grows considerably.

In the meantime, these "shepherds" lead their unusual herd to those rice fields that have been harvested in the morning; the ducks are left free to select their own food which will be later supplemented back at the farm when they are returned to their sheds.

A shepherd with his herd of a hundred or so ducks.

RESOURCES OF THE SEA

Because of the sea's resources, there are many fishermen in Bali. They still fish according to traditional methods, working side by side, always ready to provide mutual assistance. These fishermen take to the sea in their typical wooden boats (very few are equipped with a motor) and concede nothing to modern technology: even the industrially-manufactured nets have proven unsuccessful with the Balinese fishing community. The only exception are the preservation and freezing operations needed in order to be able export the fish.

When the fishermen return to shore, they engage in a Balinese ritual called *ngujur* or gathering of the fish which falls on the sand when it is being transferred from the boat to receptacles. This unique gathering activity is generally the monopoly of young boys who in exchange for their help ask the fishermen for a fish or two. In keeping with the ancient beliefs, still deeply rooted today, that maintain that giving fish will protect from harm or trouble, the superstitious fishermen generally oblige.

Fishing boats are also used to transport things or people, including those tourists eager to take part in the fishing experience.

Salt is another of the sea's product and the Balinese salt market is a flourishing one also in view of the fact that salt has many therapeutic qualities, especially those salts which are rich in iodine and used in the treatment of thyroid problems. Nonetheless, because it is seasonal, the production of salt is not particularly profitable.

The process entails collecting sea water with tools which are made from the *pelepah* of the *areca* type palms (the tools can be frequently seen in use in Kusamba Beach, near Semarapura Town, capital of Klungkung) and then letting it evaporate in the sun. It follows that during the rainy season, this activity comes to a standstill. In some cases, in order to overcome the problem, the Balinese have resorted to boiling sea water in very large kettles until it dries.

Fishermen taking to the sea in their traditional wooden boats.

A Balinese carries on his shoulders the typical tools used to collect sea water (first step in the production of salt).

A woodcarver engaged in the art of mask carving.

The difficult carving of an entire tree trunk.

WOODCARVING

Balinese woodcarving is highly appreciated by local and foreign tourists (and has contributed substantially to economic development).

A real art form, passed on from father to son, there are many renown woodcarvers on the island. Just to mention a one example, the village of Mas has gained fame thanks to its very famous master carvers.

Men generally engage in the art of woodcarving while the women add the finishing touches and coloring. The artistic production is quite varied, ranging from mythological statues to carvings of animals, flowers and fruits, all bearing a remarkable resemblance to reality even in the perfection of colors. Balinese woodcarvers are also renown for furniture which is capably carved in the shape of doors, windows and columns.

Panels carved to decorate the interior walls of homes are worthy of special mention. In this case, different kinds of wood are used such as: ebony coming from Sulawesi and Kalimantan, teak (from Java) which is best suited for panels, doors, windows and furniture, and other kinds of local wood such *sawo, panggal buaya, waru* (a type of hibiscus), *nangka*, etc.

Entire tree trunks are sometimes used when carving something too complex and difficult for an ordinary piece of wood.

The Balinese themselves are fond of this kind of art and the wealthier like to have their homes and private prayer areas decorated with woodcarvings. Wood ornaments can also be found in many of Bali's public buildings. Nonetheless, this eleborate production is, above all, destined for the tourist market.

The local authorities have, therefore, created special market areas for the woodcarvers who directly

Some objects carved out of wood: above, to the left, the elaborate face of Rangda, generally associated with the divinity of death; to the right, two woodcarvers carving musical instruments; below, a woman painting the wood objects.

Opposite, various examples of Balinese stone sculptures symbolizing the main Hindu divinities, manifestations of Ida Hyang Widi, and the two craftsmen sculpting them.

sell their production and establish the price according to the characteristics and value of each carving.

Commercial centers and art markets are thus flourishing in Bali. Nonetheless, it is not uncommon to run into carvers who continue to earn their living as farmers, employees and so on.

STONE SCULPTURES

Besides woodcarving, the Balinese are also very skillful at sculpting and engraving stone, especially the typical volcanic stone of the island.

Their sculptures, born of masterful hands, achieve the same level of quality as that of the artistic woodcarvings.

It is not by chance, therefore, that most of the temples of Bali, as well as the public buildings, are made of splendidly sculpted stone. Sculpted stone statues (generally, sacred images of the Hindu divinities) are used extensively to adorn areas of worship, but can also be found along the streets, on corners, in the

gardens and in the Balinese homes.

The tourists themselves find it difficult to resist the allure of this art form. The only thing refraining them from buying a stone sculpture seems to be the evident difficulty of shipping it home or finding a proper place for it.

PAINTING

When speaking of art, there is no denying the artistry of the famous Balinese painters. The beauty and variety of their paintings have gained the admiration of the tourists.

The island boasts many prime centers of pictoric art: Batuan, Ubud, Kamasan etc. It is in these villages that highly acclaimed local painters live and flourish, such as I Gusti Nyoman Lempad (regrettably, now deceased), Anak Agung Gede Sobrat, Ida Bagus Made, I Wayan Jata, Kobot and more. Even some well-established foreign artists have chosen to make these centers their home. They include Antonio Blanco, Arie Smit, Hans Snel, Le Mayeur, and Walter Spice (the last two have recently passsed away).

But the fame and reputation of the Balinese artists is such that their paintings are exhibited and sold in large specialized commercial centers. Their contribution to economic development and to the betterment of the standard of living of the Balinese people is undeniable.

An artist painting fruits and a bird perched on top of the leaves of a *psidium guajava.*

A painting depicting the work of the farmers in the rice fields. This is a typical product of the most affirmed pictoric current in Bali, commonly indicated as *Young Artist* whose founder was Arie Smit.

A suggestive sunset view of the cliff on which the Uluwatu Temple rises.

A view of the temple's courtyards and the gateways (*Candi Bentar*).

ULUWATU

The temple of Uluwatu, located on the South-Western coast of Bali, is dedicated to Dewa Rudra and is associated with *Nawa Sanga* (the nine manifestations of the supreme divinity). The temple is perched on a cliff in an enchanting position and is indeed ideally suited to enjoy the setting sun over the vast Indonesian ocean.

The temple itself is one of the most important in Bali. It is an area of public worship and thus open to all devoted Hindus regardless of class, profession and origin. Enormous crowds, therefore, gather here periodically to parary during the ritual ceremonies. They arrive with an abundance of offerings to invoke peace and prosperity from their god.

Like all the other large Balinese temples, Uluwatu appears to be subdivided into three courtyards: an outer one known as *jabaan,* a central one, called *jaba tengah* (with a door called *Candi Bentar* in the center) and the interior courtyard, *jeroan*. The upper part of the *Candi Bentar* has an arched form, reminiscent of the arch formed by the wings of a bird. It is rarely observed in the typical Balinese architecture. Once inside the *jeroan*, it is necessary to go through another passeway (*Candi Kurung* or *Kuri Agung*), conceived as the image of the sacred mountain Mahameru. It is flanked and guarded by two statues which represent the god Ganesh (*Dwarapala*). The *Candi Kurung* is capped by a majestic decorative figure *(Kala Head)* which has 2 eyes and a large necklace. Over the *Kala Head* is the *Guci Amertha* (source of life).

On the whole, the temple and its peculiar architecture is highly suggestive and because of its nearness to the international airport and the tourist centers in the Badung Regency (Kuta and Nusa Dua), it is a favorite destination of many organized tours.

Tourists, however, are not allowed inside the temple when the ceremonies are taking place. Otherwise, visits are subject to rigorous respect of the rules (appropriate attire, including wearing a shawl around the waist, respectful behavior etc.) and lastly, women are forbidden from entering the temple during their menstrual cycle because they are deemed to be impure.

Nonethelss, reaching Uluwatu is extremely easy: it is situated only 200 meters from a spacious parking lot.

When the tides are high, Tanah Lot is completely surrounded by the sea. The atmosphere is enchanting in the soffused light at sunset.

TANAH LOT

A truly singular and characteristic temple, Tanah Lot is built on a rocky strip of land which the high tides transform into an island, making access from the land impossible.

It is especially suggestive at sunset when the light, at times a thin thread and others, a bright flash, bounces off the waves.

Located only 27 km. from Denpasar, it is indeed a major tourist attraction. One of the *Dang Kahyangan* temples, Tanah Lot is also of great importance for the Hindu population. It is closely associated with a very venerated and charismatic priest, Dang Hyang Nirartha who came to Bali in 1489 from Madjapahit (Eastern Java). It was to be a short stay but he ended up spending the rest of his life on the island where he endeavored with the population to defend local culture and to foster respect of the spirit of the Hindu religion.

According to Hindu belief, he achieved the final dimension of the saints, called *moksa*, where the soul reaches Nirvana and can no longer be reincarnated. The Balinese culture, in fact, is enveloped in these concepts which, however, manage to blend easily with the need for progress and modern development.

As to the religious ceremonies held in Tanah Lot (often influenced by the rising tide, and at times, forcing people to pray on the adjacent shore), the faithful arrive in multitudes from all over Bali and even elsewhere. They come bearing gifts, wishing to pay homage to the greatness of Dang Hyang Nirartha, and to pray the supreme Ida Hyang Widi in order to be granted prosperity and serenity for their bodies and souls.

THE MONKEY FOREST

There are many places in Bali (especially in the forests) where monkeys live, free and undisturbed. These hundreds of monkeys are a real attraction for the tourists.

For the people of Bali, instead, these so-called "monkey forests" are actually sacred places where a temple can always be found among the trees. Likewise, each forest has its sacred tree, called *pala*, and the majestic trunk and wood cannot be touched nor, obviously, used unless natural causes force the tree to fall down. In its own way, faith is making a small contribution to the conservation of the few remaining forests in Bali.

One of the most famous Monkey Forests (besides the one called Alas Kedaton, near the village of Marga in the Tabanan Regency), is found in the Badung Regency.

Called Sangeh, and in keeping with tradition, it has a *pala* and a temple, the Taman Sari. The faithful come when ceremonies are held while the tourists flock there daily.

The authorities have stimulated tourism by building parking lots near the several roads leading to the forests. As to the tourists, they seem to enjoy walking through the forest in order to visit the temple and at the same time, feed the monkeys. But feeding the monkeys is not without its risks. Monkeys can be temperamental and rather spiteful. If the offer of food doesn't appease them, they will approach the tourist to try to grab anyone of the many objects that people normally carry.

The guards are often quite busy keeping the monkeys at bay, so caution is advised and in case of any problem, tourists should turn to the qualified personnel for help.

The monkeys after which the *Monkey Forests* are named, sacred areas for the Balinese.

The Taman Ayun Temple in Mengwi with its moat and pagodas; right, the *Dwarapala*, the large statue guarding the entrance.

THE TAMAN AYUN TEMPLE IN MENGWI

Before Indonesia became a single independent nation there were numerous kingdoms in Bali. One of these was Mengwi; and the beautiful Taman Ayun Temple was under its jurisdiction. Unique and suggestive, this fascinating temple holds a very special appeal for the many tourists who visit it.

One of its most distinctive features are the numerous pagodas or *Meru*, rising high above the interior courtyard and meant to symbolize Mahameru, the sacred mountain; according to the traditional belief, this is the residence of the supreme god and the ancestral souls, the latter arriving there after having been consacrated by the cremation *(Ngaben)* and purification *(Memukur)* ceremonies.

Inside the central courtyard stands a large statue *(Dwarapala)*, image of a giant who, with weapon in hand *(gada),* appears to be guarding the entrance. This is a customary presence in the sacred Balinese area although the entrances are generally flanked by two statues.

The Taman Ayun giant has somewhat of a demoniacal look: bulging and staring eyes, massive body,

Ritual offerings presented each day by the faithful of the Hindu community; in the background, the Taman Ayun Temple.

The Ulun Danu Temple on Lake Beratan, with two pagodas respectively, with 11 and 3 tiers.

Following pages: a very suggestive view of the Ulun Danu Temple in Bedugul.

curly hair, and the threatening *gada*.

The faithful come to Taman Ayun in great numbers, from all over Mengwi, to pay homage to the greatness of its ancient kings and to express their devotion to the supreme god and his manifestations. The presence of tourists is also steady and numerous. They can easily reach the temple although they are not allowed to go beyond the outer courtyard for a closer look at the temple's beauty. Nonetheless, even a peaceful walk around the outer walls (surrounded by a moat whose water comes from a nearby river) is equally rewarding and affords rare and suggestive glimpses.

THE ULUN DANU TEMPLE

The Ulun Danu Temple is situated along Lake Beratan, at Bedugul, in the Tabanan Regency. A beautiful setting with nearby mountains providing crisp and clear air, and a marvelous panorama are just a few of the elements that attract the multitude of tourists.

As in the case of the Taman Ayun Temple, Ulun Danu flourishes with an array of pagodas or *Meru* characterized by the multi-tiered roofs.

Meru is basically the sacred residence (*sthana*) either of the omnipresent god Ida Hyang Widi and his many manifestations or of the ancestral spirits, especially those having great merits.

The various tiers of the pagodas refer to the different known manifestations of Ida Hyang Widi. Consequently, when the *Meru* is consacrated as the residence of Ida Hyang Widi only, pagodas are found having 3, 5, 7, 9, and 11 tiers; they correspond respectively to the different types of manifestations; that is, to the Tri-murti, to the *Panca Dewata* (5 representations), to *Sapta Dewata* (7), to *Nawa Sanga* (9), and to *Ekadasa Rudra* (11).

If the *Meru,* instead, is considered the sacred shelter (*sthana*) of the ancestral spirits only, the number of tiers are meant to reflect the social class to whom the *Meru* is dedicated.

The Ulun Danu Temple represents the vivifying forces of the lake whose waters provide fertility and make it possible to develop the nearby cultivations. It is, in fact, consacrated to Dewi Danu, goddess of the lake and manifestation of the supreme divinity to whom the faithful, especially the farmers, bring offerings and invoke well being and prosperity. As to the tourists, as in other cases, they can only go as far as the outer courtyard.

Goa Gajah, better known as the Elephant Cave.

Following pages: the large basin near the Elephant Cave and the six anthropomorphous statues which are also fountains.

THE ELEPHANT CAVE

Bali has much to offer, including something for the archeologists. One such example is the famous "Elephant Cave" (*Goa Gajah*); an inscription found at the base on the right side of its gateway makes it possible to trace it approximately back to the XIth Century. Most likely, it was a complex sacred structure used for prayer as well as for meditation and ascetic practices. It is believed that the faithful of the Hindu and Buddhist religions gathered here; likewise, it is certain that the sacredness of the area has been maintained since even now rites are celebrated here and attended by people from all over the island who bring gifts and gather in prayer.

The Elephant Cave is structurally interesting; the gateway appears to be framed by a beautiful decorated relief where figures, animals and plants are entwined. Inside, there are 15 niches of different sizes and shapes. In the most western one, stands the statue of Ganesh while on the eastern side, to the east, there are 3 *lingga*, phallic symbols of the god Siwa. Two statues that typically guard sacred places tower over the cave's opening (*Dwarapala*). About 5 meters from the entrance an usual element stands out - a large stone basin with 6 monumental statues and water gushing forth. The entire complex is perfectly preserved (the statues were restored in 1954). Most likely, it is there that the faithful went to cleanse and purify their hands and face before withdrawing to meditate.

The authorities of the central government and the local administration were quick to realize the potential of the *Goa Gajah* complex and have made substantial contributions to its conservation. Steps have been taken to promote cultural tourism, and in this way, the Elephant Cave has become an important destination for foreign and local tourists, especially during school vacation. The Elephant Cave has come to represent a important factor for the culture and history of the island and as well as one that contributes to the economic development of the region.

A detail of the interesting stone relief of Yeh Pulu, found near Bedulu and *Goa Gajah*.

A suggestive view of the green shores of the Pakerisan River which flows along the cleft that opens up like a door on the side of Mount Gunung Kawi.

GUNUNG KAWI

The Gunung Kawi Sanctuary, like the *Goa Gajah,* dates back to the XIth Century. It sits in a beautiful panoramic setting and is visited daily by tourists who come not only for the lush natural setting but for the monuments that stand out as a symbol of culture.

Special parking areas have been created for the tourists who also have the option of a stairway leading to sacred area.

The sanctuary is directly associated with the memory of King Anak Wungsu, noble son of King Udayana Warmadewa and to Queen Mahendradatta, who governed from 1049 to 1077. This historical information is known because of the text on the sanctuaries, called *Haji lumah ing Jalu.* The Gunung Kawi sanctuary is still used today for ritual ceremonies and the local population gathers here periodically to offer the usual gifts, to pay homage to the ancient king and his family, and to pray the gods.

Previous pages: Gunung Kawi or Temple of the cut rock, an area of meditation and prayer.

The *Tirta Empul* or Water of the sacred spring, a sacred area near Tampaksiring.

The Hindu population normally cleanses itself by entering the sacred waters flowing from inside the sanctuary.

TIRTA EMPUL

The village of Tampaksiring, in the Gianyar Regency, is situated near Gunung Kawi. It is known for the presence of *Tirta Empul* (a name which more or less means "spring water" or "source of water") and is a place of worship found inside the Temple (Temple of the source of sacred water). Understandably, as the name implies, the spring water is considered sacred and used in the religious ceremonies. Many indeed are the faithful who come here to cleanse themselves in keeping with the belief that by purifying their body they are also purifying their spirit.

The sacred water also attracts hoards of tourists, especially during vacation season. Assisting them is a capable organization, established by the central government as well as the local population who is anxious to enhance their cultural wealth. Tourists are allowed into the religious area and may take pictures as long as their behaviour is appropriate and respectful of the sacredness of the temple.

Previous pages: above, the interior of Tirta Empul. Below, one of the sacred basins used for the purifying bath.

The part of the temple consacrated to Surya, sun god, called *Padmasana*.

Opposite, the large Seribatu complex; in the forefront, the large basin fed by numerous water spouts. As can be seen, the different structures blend naturally and actually enhance the lush vegetation surrounding them.

Following pages: children happily swimming in the large sacred pool. One of the gargoyles which feed the pool with gushing water.

SERIBATU

Seribatu, near Tagallalang, in the Gianyar Regency, is decidedly a very particular place. It attracts visitors and tourists for its charming natural scenery, its clean and crisp air, and its incredibly clean and well taken care of environs. People here live in large homes or farms and are especially skillful in woodcarving.

Seribatu has a temple which, in many ways, has a structure very similar to that of *Tirta Empul* (or Temple of the water of the sacred spring). The large sacred complex includes several sanctuaries, including the one known as *Padmasana*. It is made of stone and bricks, and is consacrated to Surya or Aditya (sun god), a very venerated divinity because it is identified with the supreme Siwi.

Many faithful come here on a pilgrimage, and regardless of their family, class, origin or profession, they all stop in prayer before the sanctuary after having offered gifts as a token of gratitude.

Even in Seribatu, right in front of the temple, there is a large basin fed by numerous water jets. It here that in a typically ritual gesture, the faithful wet themselves with the water for water is not only the basis of mankind's existence; for the Balinese water has a profound spiritual and sacred significance.

Understandably, the faithful Hindu are not the only ones to visit the temple of Seribatu. Many are the tourists who come to visit the complex, to rest and to acquire strength in this peaceful setting. Nonetheless, the greatest appeal comes from the numerous sanctuaries dedicated to Ida Hyang Widi and his manifestations and to the ancestral spirits. These sanctuaries stand out for the elaborate workmanship and for the shiny painted golden finish.

A panoramic view of the area of Kintamani dominated by the massive volcano, Mount Batur and the lake spread out at its feet.

KINTAMANI

The district of Kintamani, in the Bangli Regency, is dominated by a massive mountain, Mount Batur, which is still an active volcano. A violent eruption in 1917 destroyed some 2500 temples as well as a vast number of homes and even entire villages.

Mount Batur, like Mount Agung in the Karangasem Regency and Batukaru, in Tabanan, is considered a sacred mountain by the Hindu population of Bali. Its eruption, however, did not only cause death and destruction but ironically had a positive side: the slopes of the mountain and the areas surrounding it (where the large Lake Batur is) have turned out to be extraordinarily fertile thanks to the vivifying effect of the ashes and volcanic matter. The area has become

very productive for the growing of oranges, banana trees and coffee plants.

Many villages are disseminated at the foot of the mountain: Songan, Toya Bungkah, Kedisan, Abang and Trunyan.

The latter holds a special appeal for the tourists who come to enjoy the very pleasant climate, the natural beauties as well as very unique custom perpetuated by the villagers: not only do they not cremate the bodies of their dead, they do not even bury them. They are simply left on a stone platform in the village cemetery.

If the tourists seek a lighter form of entertainment, they can take a boat trip around the lake, now that motorboats are finally available here.

LAKE BATUR

Lake Batur is a vast expanse of calm water, situated at the foot of the volcano. Many small villages dot its shores and the local population is basically made up of farmers and fishermen. Nonetheless, they have readily perceived the needs of tourism and its inherent benefits. Restaurants and hotels have made their appearance, along with the first motorboats. The local fishermen, instead, still rely on traditional rowboats known as *bedau* from which they cast their nets or their fishing-lines and hooks.

The importance of the lake for local economy is easily understandable. For this reason, the government authorities periodically restock the lake with fish. For the local populations, the lake is a precious source of drinking water and is also used to irrigate their fields where cabbage and other vegetables are grown.

The sacred Ulun Danu Temple rises on the lake's shore and it is here that the Hindu from all over Bali converge for the religious ceremonies and to perform their devotional rituals.

Left, the characteristic Kintamani Temple.

View of Lake Batur and outlined in the background, the volcano bearing the same name. Evident are the traditional boats used by the fishermen with their extremely rudimentary methods of obtaining water for everyday use.

The Besakih Temple with its numerous minor temple and Mount Agung in the background. Below, some devotees gathered in prayer as the priest offers them sacred water.

Following pages: a comprehensive view of the Besakih complex. The typical gateway can be observed on the right.

BESAKIH

Besakih rises from the South-Western slope of Mount Agung,, the most sacred and revered mountain by the Balinese population. It is the largest temple of the Hindu religion. Actually, it is a vast complex grouping together 18 minor temples and 17 *pedharman* directly associated with the three largest nuclei which correspond to the three supreme manifestations of Ida Hyang Widi: in the center, the Penataran Agung Temple, consacrated to Siwa; to the north, the Batu Madeg Temple for Wisnu; and to the south, the Kiduling Kreteg Temple for Brahma.

The Penataran Agung Temple, in turn, has in its nucleus three *Padmasana (Padmasana Tiga)*, dedicated respectively to Parama Siwa, Sada Siwa and Siwa. It is here that the most important and suggestive ceremonies are held.

The great Besakih complex grew gradually, layer after layer, at the hands of the whole Balinese population. Today, it is considered a *Kahyangan Jagat,* a public temple for all the Hindus of Indonesia. Multitudes of faithful converge here to participate in the ceremonies, to offer gifts, to seek peace and prosperity, never failing to make contributions for the conservation and restoration (if necessary) of the many parts of the temple.

The most important religious ceremonies takes place once every 100 years called *Ekadasa Rudra*, every 10 years called *Panca Wali Krama* and every year in October, when the moon is full, called *Piodalalan*. The air is permeated with solemnity and a sense of absolute communion between body and spirit which the faithful Hindu are capable of achieving when in the presence of the omnipresent Ida Hyang Widi.

The tourists arrive here by following the customary travel agency itineraries or after having heard about the ceremony from their hotel or other information centers, and are instantly spell-bound by the atmosphere of this suggestive ceremony. That notwithstanding, they can only assist from the most outer zone of the temple. But they can always admire the many beautiful natural settings and breathe in the invigorating air of a 1000-meter altitude.

The Kehen Temple in Bangli has some very peculiar features.
Firstly, the ornamental reliefs which are extremely elaborate and
sculpted in stone (on the right, a detail of a *makara* which
undeniably looks like an elephant). Then the stairway leading to
the door (*Candi Kurung* or *Kuri Agung*), punctuated by statues
representing the characters of *Ramayana,* symmetrically located
to the right and left.

Following pages: the central nucleus of the Kehen Temple,
partially restored and partly characterized by buildings which
look traditional and which, instead, are recent constructions.

THE KEHEN TEMPLE
IN BANGLI

In the center of the city of Bangli, half-way up the
mountain, rises the Kehen Temple, one of the most
ancient and suggestive temples in Bali. From an inscription, it can be established that the temple dates
back to 1204 and this is also serves to indicate the
kind of reverent behavior required for the ceremonies held here.

The name *Kehen*, which currently refers to a building used as a warehouse, comes from the name of a
small temple located right in front of the large one.

The inclined position of the temple along the slope
of the mountain has actually forced the three courtyards to be on three different levels, each connected
by wide stairway.

The temple's prestige (Kehen is still considered the
religious center of the entire Bangli Regency) comes
from being very ancient as well as from the fact that
the most important religious ceremonies have been
held here and continued to be held here.

The monumental complex of Kertagosa in the center of an artificial pond is famous for the elegantly painted ceilings in the *wayang* style (opposite page, two especially significant details).

Following pages: a truly unique and suggestive bird's eye view of the painted ceiling of Kertagosa

The Balinese come in great numbers, with their usual offerings of gifts, but they are also willing to make substantial contributions for the conservation of the entire complex.

Distinctive features such as eleborate decorations and stone-sculpted reliefs, unique architectural structures, the large *Meru*, the wide stairways, the sculptures and the majestic fig tree from which the ritual wooden drum *(kulkul)* hangs make this temple one of the favorite tourist destinations year-round.

The presence of *kulkul* is customary: each *Bale Banjar* has one. Its serves to underscore the different moments of the ritual as well as all the activities that unfold in the sacred complex and which concern the entire community, such as meetings of the faithful and everything else they do to mutually assist mutually eachother.

KLUNGKUNG

Klungkung is the ancient name of the capital of the Klungkung Regency, today known as Semarapura. At the time of the kingdom, it was actually capital of all of Bali.

Since it is situated along the road leading to the Besakih Temple or to Karangasem, many local and foreign tourists headed there, will stop in Klungkung.

Its main attraction is Kertagosa, an ancient building located in the center of the city which plays an important role in the development of the region's cultural tourism. The building, an ancient hall of justice, is surrounded by an artificial pond; its ceilings are elaborately painted with scenes depicting exemplary punishment (perhaps as a source of inspiration for the judges questioning the prisoners) as well as scenes taken from *Mahabharata* and the Indonesian version of *Ramayana*: some characters, such as the servant Penakawan, are not found in the original Indian tale, while they are a part of Balinese culture (Penakawan, in particular, in the dances inspired by the two poems, represents he who can translate ancient Javanese or *kawi* into the language of Bali). The pictoric style of these paintings is so peculiar that it has been given a specific denomination - the Kamasan style, a name which comes from a village located 4 kilometers south of the city of Semarapura.

It is still possible today to meet numerous painters in Kamasan with their traditional tools (ranging from bamboo brushes to mineral colors); they still engage in this ancient and precious art and pass it on to others.

The tourists visit the village after having admired at length the precious painted ceilings in Kertagosa; here, another artistically-important element stands out: a large winged lion made out of wood and called Singa Ambara. It is a mythological animal which in this particular instance, serves a more earthly function: it is the base of the column which bears the weight of the building's entire roof.

The Goa Lawah Temple (or Bat Cave) with thousands of these animals who have chosen to make their home here.

Following pages: a priest wearing the ritual white vestments distributes sacred water, considered a form of blessing of the supreme Ida Hyang Widi, to the faithful gathered in prayer.

THE GOA LAWAH TEMPLE

Many visitors like to spend a few hours in Kusamba Beach, in the Klungkung Region; they are attracted by the sea and the possibility of watching the various traditional salt collecting operations which take place right on the beach.

Once there, it's hard to resist the temptation of visiting a one-of-a-kind spot, located right near the road leading to Kusamba Beach: the Goa Lawah Temple or the Bat Cave (*goa* - cave and *lawah* - bat).

The unmistakable name comes from the fact that this large sacred complex rises right in front of a cave where literally thousands of bats hang peacefully from its walls, napping until the time comes to take off in flight, generally at night, to go look for food.

It should be pointed out that in Bali, the bat is considered a sacred animal in spite of the fact that there are those Balinese who habitually enjoy the taste of its meat.

It's not surprising, at any rate, that a number of small temples consacrated to the supreme Ida Hyang Widi and his numerous manifestations and to the ancestral spirits, rise right in front of the cave.

The entire sacred complex is one of the region's most important religious sites since it includes one of the *Sad Kahyangan* temples (the 6 public temples open to everyone in Bali). It is located at the southern end and is looked upon as a sacred site of Brahma.

During the ceremonies, the faithful Hindu converge here to pray and receive from the priests the sacred water or *tirta* which, according to tradition, is also a way to gain the blessing of Ida Hyang Widi.

Proof of the fact that not only the faithful come here is the large parking lot built near the temple as well as the abundance of kiosks and stands selling products of local crafts, fruits and other objects all obviously destined to meet the needs of the tourists.

An aerial view of the renown Sanur Beach, large and fashionable
Balinese tourist resort.

SANUR BEACH

The resources of the most famous tourist resorts in
Bali, are anything but religious, especially Sanur
Beach. Here, the main attractions are the beaches
with their very white sand and the beauty of con-
stantly calm waters, ideal for swimming.

At the heart of the area's tourist development is a
solid network of infrastructures which make Sanur an
atypical place in Bali: luxury hotels, refined restaurants, large commercial centers, neat and well cared
for residential districts, art galleries, chains of shops,
an efficient transportation system, and everything
else that can make the tourist's stay a total pleasure.

Just to give an exact idea of the resort's potential, it
should be emphasized that Sanur discovered its

tourist vocation only at the beginning of the sixties which is more or less when the large Ngurah Rai airport was being built along with Sanur's first truly international hotel: the Bali Beach. The hotel was entirely financed by the Japanese government as partial restitution for the damage and destruction caused when they attacked Indonesia in 1942 during World War II.

After this first large hotel was built, tourist development in Bali continued at a steady rate and without obstacles. It has continued to grow also thanks to substantial and well planned investments which not only served to build the hotel but to implement the kind of network of services that Sanur is renown for.

An aerial view of the Nusa Dua zone with the two islands which give the resort its name.
Opposite, a suggestive sunset view.

Two examples of Nusa Dua's tourist attractions: above, a swimming pool surrounded by vegetation; below, a large golf course.

NUSA DUA

Located a short distance from the international airport (approximately 10 km. only) and connected to nearby Sanur Beach by a very nice highway, Nusa Dua is a pleasant enclave exclusively dedicated to tourism.

Built in the mid-eighties with funds from the International Monetary Fund, Nusa Dua sits at the end of the Bukit Peninsula, in the southern part of Bali. In the local language Nusa Dua literally means "two islands" and the resort is actually located on two islands which are artificially connected to the mainland and which can be easily reached.

Conceived to meet all the demands of tourism, this famous resort offers the best in terms of tourist structures and services: large and very efficient hotel complexes, swimming pools surrounded by the lush vegetation, well-kept, large golf courses where international competitions are also held, exclusive beaches for tourists only and many fashionable shops.

On the whole, Nusa Dua is an ultramodern and well planned village, but it also reflects the outstanding levels of beauty achieved by contemporary Balinese architecture.

107

Two eloquent images of Kuta Beach where recently-built tourists infrastructures blend well with the traditional Balinese landscape.

Following pages: three very significant views of Kuta Beach at sunset: from the suggestive natural atmosphere to the cozy and lively bars, pubs, and restaurants.

KUTA BEACH

As in the case of Sanur and Nusa Dua, Kuta Beach is a true pearl in the Balinese tourist structure. But while Nusa Dua was created above all with a network of luxury international hotels ideally equipped for the international circuit, Kuta Beach has succeeded in creating the kind of tourist ambience that is capable of meeting the needs of everyone, from the foreigners to the locals. And the local population along with the Indonesian businessmen have all been involved in this endeavor.

The people of Kuta Beach are truly at ease in dealing with the foreigners and have capably managed to benefit by exploiting all the local attractions such as the religious and folkloristic events which are extremely well organized and suggestive. They have built beautiful temples and well preserved the older ones, regardless of whether they belong to the whole village or to a single family.

As to the local families, they generally live in beautiful and spacious homes which they will gladly trans-form into a sort of hostel for paying guests who want to spend more time here.

The local economy therefore is healthy and growing. It is backed by a network of shops where visitors can purchase all kinds of artistic objects and products of crafts at all kinds of prices: the choice varies from simple souvenirs to the kind of art that can be found in the galleries of the regions of Mas and Ubud, in the Gianyar Regency. In keeping with a popular practice, the sale is left open to negotiation. The only exceptions are the large department stores which display their prices, after having applied large discounts. Negotiations come easy in Bali because every seller speaks many languages: English, French, Italian, Japanese.

If the tourist wants to buy a typical item from another area outside Bali and doesn't have the time to go there, the problem is easily solved: in Bali, they will find products made in Kalimantan, Sumatra, Java, Sumbawa, Sumba, Irian Jaya and elsewhere.

JIMBARAN BEACH

There is another resort near Kuta Beach and the international airport which the tourists are quite fond of. It Jimbaran Beach and it affords marvelous sunsets over the sea and interesting glimpses of traditional fishing activities. Once a simple fishing village, it has become a tourist resort with many affordable hotels and restaurants. The beaches are bustling with joggers in the morning, afternoon and in the sunset's suggestive light.

As to the fishermen, they still generally use their traditional wooden boats and only a few of them have now resorted to sails and motors. They have, however, learned to cater to the tourists and for a fee will take them out on their boats , teach them something about local sailing and offer a closer look at the beauty of their sea. This too is a small but important contribution to the economy of the entire community.

Jogging is a widely practiced sport in Jimbaran Beach and is especially enticing in the soffused light of sunset.

The beaches not only bustle with tourists but with the young locals and their typical boats.

Upon returning to shore, the fruits of an entire day of fishing are gathered.

The many stores selling gadgets, souvenirs and products of the crafts, created in the main tourist centers, display the entire array of their merchandise in a feast of colors.

Another comprehensive view of the products which can be purchased in Balinese shops: clothing, paintings, leather or silver objects, and the classic wooden puppets (*wayang golek*).

SHOPPING

For the tourists visiting the most reknown Balinese resorts, shopping in definitely one of their favorite activities. From their part, the local populations have greatly endeavored to meet their every need. The end result has been the development of many typical and bustling markets where visitors can buy any- and everything, from the typical products of local craftsmen to other highly sought products from near-by areas (for example, the famous Javanese puppets, known as *wayang golek*).

Worthy of special mention are the markets, the stores and the multitude of stalls in Kuta Beach where the tourist is literally engulfed by a flood of clothing ranging from T-shirts to slacks, all characterized by vivacious and bright colors, made of either silk or cotton, printed or hand embroidered with very orginal patterns and designs.

In the course of the years, the products sold in Kuta Beach have become so popular that many boutiques have been set up and each one now offers its own personal line of styles. This, in general, has contributed to the economy of Bali and, in particular, to the development of tourism.

The area of Ubud is especially well equipped to cater to the tourists who come, attracted by the natural setting. Part of Ubud's fame however comes from a school of paiting which originated here and which is beautifully illustrated above.

THE TOURIST AREA OF UBUD

The area of Ubud, in the Gianyar Regency, is well known and above all appreciated as an art center having its own typical style of painting. The works of art of the Ubud school can be admired in the museum or in the many local art galleries.

Needless to say, tourists are readily attracted to this art center and this has undoubtedly benefited the area's economy. Many hotels have been built around Ubud, as well as picturesque inns; such a choice of accomodations is sure to satisfy everyone's wallet.

Tourists, therefore, generally tend to spend several days in Ubud, equally attracted by a number of rather well preserved monuments and the almost daily artistic performances staged especially for their benefit.

In spite of this massive presence of visitors, the local population is not at all distracted from its religious and devotional duties. At the same time, the entire community of Ubud is deeply committed to maintaining a clean and tranquil community.

The water falls of Bali are a wonderful opportunity to cool off while its rivers are ideal for rafting.

SOBEK RAFTING

A unique sport which has become popular in the last five years, rafting entails traveling along a tumultous and irregular river course in a rubber raft.

The sport is ideal for people of all ages; up to 6 people can sit in the raft which runs the rapids for a couple of hours. It's also a rare opportunity to admire the most varied scenery: from thick entwined forests to the scenes of everyday life that unfolds along the river's shores.

In Bali, there is a river which is outstanding for its course and the many beautiful spots it crosses, and has thus been singled out as the ideal river for this sport. It is the Ayung River. Located 8 km. from Ubud, the Ayung is now explored by numerous tourists. They are organized in groups and led by a highly specialized guide.

The Ayung River offers 11 km. which are navigable and broken up into 22 sections of rapids. The landscape is mountainous and the river unwinds through suggestive volcanic rocks.

A number of restaurants and villages of bungalows have cropped up nearby the river. This trend will not readily change since the Ayung River has also been included in the official circuit of international rafting events.

A farmer carrying the classic bamboo baskets on his shoulders; eight girls wearing typical costumes, hair adorned with fresh flowers (generally, white jasmin and red hibiscus) and small gold corollas, rest after having placed their offerings before the temple.

A dancer playing Rangda, without his mask but with his typical costume made of three colors: red, sacred for Brahma, black for Wisnu and white, the color of Siwa. Below, a woman carrying offerings to the temple. Her intense facial expression reveals a psychological state very similar to a trance which is often observed in the faithful during religious ceremonies.

THE BALINESE

The people of Bali, with their colorful and picturesque costumes, their spectacular events and traditional activities, are themselves a major attraction and one that fascinates the tourists.

They are indeed an often sought photo opportunity. So it is that tourist can be seen taking pictures of the farmers returning home after a hard day's work in the fields or rice paddies, carrying large bamboo baskets on their shoulders with forage for the animals, or the girls draped in their simple but very colorful costumes (consisting of a cloth wrapped around their body and held at the waist with a shawl)on their way to the temples with their offerings of fruit and flowers set on a silver platter, or the dancers with their woodcarved masks, or the young man leading his herd of ducks out to pasture. That is to say, that in every corner of Bali, tourists can uncover a welcome surprise.

Some more images of the people of Bali: a girl with votive offerings; a boy leading a herd of ducks; a woman wearing her everyday white dress consisting of a jacket and *sarong*; a dancer.

JAVA

MENJANGAN ISLAND

BALI SEA

Ketapang

Mt. Prapat
310
Banyuwedang   Sumberkerta

Gilimanuk   Pulaki

Lovina

S. Banyupoh

Celukanbawang   Seririt

Grokgak   Pengastulan

Banyuwangi

Mt. Kelatakan
698

Mt. Sangian
1004
Mt. Merbuk
1386

Mt. Mesehe
1344

Mt. Musi
1224

West Bali National Park

Mt. Patas
1580

S. Melaya

S. Sangiang

S. Daya

S. Suba

S. Mendaun

Melaya

S. Daya

Bilukpoh

Yeh Sumbul

Pulukan

Pupuan

Cupel   Negera

Mendaya

Cape Perancak   Perancak

Pulukan

Yehbatian

Antosari

Soka

MYANMAR
(BURMA)

LAOS

MUANG THAI

VIET
NAM

KÂMPÚCHÉA

PILIPINAS

PACIFIC

OCEAN

KEPULAUAN
TALAUD

MALAYSIA

BRUNEI

KEPULAUAN
BUNGURAN

KALIMANTAN
(BORNEO)

KEPULAUAN
SANGIHE

HALMAHERA

PULAU
BIAK

PULAU
YAPEN

IRIAN
JAYA

PAPUA
NEW GUINEA

SINGAPURA

PULAU
SIMEULUE

PULAU
NIAS

SUMATERA

PULAU
BANGKA

I   N   D   O   N   E   S   I   A

SULAWESI
(CELEBES)

CERAM

PULAU
BURU

KEPULAUAN
KAI

KEPULAUAN
ARU

PULAU
DOLAK

KEPULAUAN
MENTAWAI

PULAU
BELITUNG

PULAU
BUTUNG

PULAU
FLORES

BALI

JAVA

PULAU LOMBOK

PULAU SUMBAWA

PULAU
SUMBA

PULAU
TIMOR

KEPULAUAN
TANIMBAR

INDIAN

OCEAN

AUSTRALIA

I   N